MW00526214

DAME EVELYN GLENNIE is the first person in history to successfully create and sustain a full-time career as a solo percussionist, performing worldwide with the greatest orchestras, conductors and artists. She fondly recalls having played the first percussion concerto in the history of The Proms at the Albert Hall in 1992, which paved the way for orchestras around the world to feature percussion concerti. She had the honour of a leading role in the Opening Ceremony of the London 2012 Olympic Games.

Evelyn regularly provides masterclasses and consultations designed to guide the next generation. She is also a leading commissioner of over 200 new pieces for solo percussion for many of the world's most eminent composers. The film 'Touch the Sound' and her enlightening TED speech remain key testimonies to her approach to sound-creation.

Evelyn was awarded an OBE in 1993 and now has nearly 100 international awards to date, including the Polar Music Prize and the Companion of Honour. Evelyn continues to inspire and motivate people from all walks of life. Her masterclasses and consultations are designed to guide the next generation.

Evelyn is currently embarking on the formation of the Evelyn Glennie Archive Collection. The vision is to open a centre that embodies her mission to *Teach the World to Listen*. She aims to 'improve communication and social cohesion by encouraging everyone to discover new ways of listening. We want to inspire, to create, to engage and to empower'.

LISTEN WORLD!

EVELYN GLENNIE

The World's Premier Solo Percussionist

Hearing
Others'
Voices

BALESTIER PRESS
LONDON · SINGAPORE

Balestier Press
Centurion House, Staines-upon-Thames TW18 4AX, United Kingdom
www.balestier.com

Listen World!
Copyright © Evelyn Glennie, 2019

First published by Balestier Press in 2019

A CIP catalogue record for this book
is available from the British Library.

ISBN 978 1 911221 64 7

All rights reserved. No part of this publication may be
reproduced, stored in a retrieval system or transmitted in
any form or by any means, electronic, mechanical, without
the prior written permission of the publisher of this book.

To Ron Forbes, my peripatetic percussion

teacher at school who opened my body to sound,

and with thanks to all the people who have touched

my life in so many ways and who have allowed me

to realize that we all have a story to tell.

My vision is a society where communication and social cohesion are improved by the act of listening.

Contents

Foreword by Keith Howard and Michael Verde   13

Preface   19

Beginnings   23

Freedom in percussion   35

The vibrating hearing body   57

To feel, to connect, to truly listen   69

The ring of words, the sound of music   93

What makes us human?   111

Listen, world, to the sound of the universe   119

You might also like   123

References   125

Questions for discussion, reflection and action   131

Foreword

by Keith Howard and Michael Verde

Keith Howard

Feel the music! Listening to music uses our whole body, which, perhaps, is why we describe music as being hot or cold, passionate, sensual. When we're tired, music helps calm us down, releasing tension built up over a long and difficult day; when we need to concentrate, we put on the radio or a recording of music, softly, in the background, to help us concentrate (and to cancel out the noises of everyday life). Music is transformative and transporting. It is magical, mesmerising, yet meaningful. Music heals and calms, and is both profound and personal. It is a universal attribute of man, since every society on earth has music. In this immensely personal book, Evelyn Glennie asks us to listen with our whole being to the magic of music

Keith Howard is professor emeritus of music at SOAS, University of London

* * *

Michael Verde

I met Evelyn Glennie while producing a documentary on listening to people with dementia.

When I asked her if she would contribute to the project, I presented her with two options. One, we could interview her talking about how she listens. Pretty simple. Or, two, we could film her meeting people with dementia and see if her gift of listening would be able to cross such a cognitive divide.

She replied at once: "The second option is very interesting. I've never met a person with dementia before."

That was her answer. And so that's what we went with—option two.

Evelyn met ten people with dementia over two days in care homes outside of London. All ten men and women were experiencing significant degrees of dementia—indeed, all were in hospice care. Several spoke; most did not. None communicated in what would pass as "normal" conversation. The families of all were open to Evelyn meeting their loved one, of course.

The idea of using music to reach people with dementia is not new. Musical memory frequently endures longer than our recall of words. But we were not asking Evelyn to make music to quicken memory. We asked her to use an even more powerful bridge than music for connecting with others: paying attention. She was welcome to bring an instrument to the visits, we told her, but we were interested in seeing if her remarkable way of resonating with her audiences and tuning into the "non-verbal" world would be effective in reaching people with impaired cognition.

Here's what I learned from Evelyn Glennie about listening in that rather remarkable context.

Real listening takes real courage: the courage to risk leaving the familiar and enter into awkward spaces; the courage to step out of one's armor and become vulnerable; the courage to take real interest in the life of another person as it matters to that person and not only as it matters to oneself; and, finally, the courage to open one's heart to the people who the world often closes its doors to and invite them to teach us how to hear what we might not expect and what we possibly even fear.

For over ten hours I watched Evelyn Glennie walk into the lives of people who many people probably believed were beyond reach and offer them all of her attention. Not every meeting was magic—magic wasn't the point; emotional connection was. But in every meeting, except one—the dear lady remained fast asleep—I witnessed how one person can bridge another person back to life by listening to him or her. Seeing these interactions brought home to me how much healing and listening are the same art. Because of the way that Evelyn was paying attention to these men and women, they came to trust her—trust that she really did care and was genuinely interested in him or her; and not as a patient or even as "a person with dementia," but as the absolutely unique person that he or she was. Being listened to like that, with all of Evelyn's attention, was healing for these men and women. You could see it in their faces and movements, hear it in their voices. It was as if you were watching people slowly begin to believe that they were human again. The change was that dramatic, that unmistakeable, and that inspiring to all present.

I've never met anyone who listens with as much of herself—mind, body, and heart—as does Dame Evelyn Glennie. Her listening is a bridge, a profound and self-giving attentiveness that can heal what can't be cured. I was blessed to learn from Evelyn what it means to truly listen, and I trust you will be as well.

Michael Verde is founder of Memory Bridge

Preface

Growing up, I was lucky enough to have experienced nature, space, clean-air and the sense of balance that comes from this. I have also been in the privileged position of comparing this to some of the most populated and polluted environments in the world.

Living and working with these extremes has helped me realize that no matter where we are from, what our environment is we all have a need to connect with each other.

How can this real connection happen? The act of listening.

As a percussionist I listen in a certain way, as musician I listen in a certain way, as a sound-creator I listen to something that is yet unknown...I wait.

This book is an invitation to tap into the wonders of listening, what that means to you and everything you engage in. What happens when you engage with the chatter in your head? When you travel to school or college? Is listening only about sound or can our whole body be a resonating chamber? Is listening about observing?

How can we begin to enhance our relationship to 'listening' and how can it influence all the decisions you make from minute to minute?

My experience is that listening is an activity that never sleeps…even when we are asleep we continue to listen! What an opportunity we have to re-engage, rethink, revisit our everyday lives to make what we do much more vivid and meaningful, and as a result, feel part of the wonders of the world?'

Evelyn Glennie
Cambridgeshire, UK
May 2019

LISTEN WORLD!

Beginnings

Follow your instincts and believe in yourself even when others don't.

It's hard to say why I took up this amazing thing called percussion. It's a question I'm asked frequently.

To tell the truth, I hadn't come across those sounds as I grew up, a farm child, in north-east Scotland.

But rhythm was everywhere. Clock ticks, heart beats, the spurts of the blood as it moves round the body, sap as it rises in the springtime trees, the clangs of iron on iron by Handel's fine blacksmith's, plants thrusting through the earth. Our breathing too, the very stuff of life. The treads as we walk, oscillations of our swinging arms. And they say that when we hear a piece of music our hearts listen and turn to beat in time, as most certainly our breathing does.

Perhaps my interest in 'percussion' began from when I heard a young girl playing a xylophone— she was brilliant. I'd had no idea a xylophone could sound like *that*.

Then when I went to school, I learned that there were many, many more percussion instruments of different shapes and sizes. What's more, I discovered that there are 600 or more objects that can be squeezed, shaken, struck or rattled to make music.

Music, that miracle of sound.

Then there are stamps and claps that come into play right at the beginning of our sound making lives!

Sound is a part of every human act. Even striking

a piece of trash with a couple of sticks and a bit of imagination can make music.

Just try for yourself, you never know ...

The world is an orchestra and we are all players in it!

Whenever found a new instrument, I explored it as a child might, all round it, under and over it, with bare hands, with sticks in my hand, searching for its heartbeat, its secret vibrations and inner energy, to create a new sound palette for performance into play.

There was no truly rational reason. But part of the reason had to be that I'd always been intrigued by music. Even as a small child I insisted on trying a plethora (more secondary level language?) of different instruments. And I loved to practice. But still, why choose a family of instruments that could not easily fit into your pocket or a bag?

I remember a vivid, early encounter with percussion. I knew I needed something else to go alongside my piano playing, which was progressing well and which was my main instrument at the time.

And then—*wham!* I mean *bang*. At aged 12, I saw my school orchestra playing during one assembly. The percussion!

It was an inexplicable feeling but as soon as I saw the percussion section I knew.

I knew that this was the family I belonged to.

* * *

There I was…not the tallest person in the world, deaf and I was entering the world of percussion; entering a sound world that I did not know; with all the complexities of tuning and frequencies. Was this going to be possible for me to do?

But even at that age, I could be persistent and stubborn, focused and independent ("Believe in yourself, yes, even if others don't", I'd got that from my father). Already I knew the score (excuse the pun) and was determined, even against all, the odds, to make it as a musician. Well you have to be, don't you, when you've discovered your passion? No other option. And, don't forget, if you do, it will pay off!

So—I still remember the smell of the tiny annexe room where my first 'trial' percussion lesson took place. I remember the ecstatic feeling of picking up and loosely, familiarly, holding a pair of drum sticks. Then—wow!—striking a snare drum for the very first time.

Immediately, immediately, I fell in love with it and, to this day, that first drum has a special place in my entire collection of over two thousand instruments along with a pair of drum sticks and a drum pad.

It was about this time that I started my fascination with trinkets which later led on to my love of jewelry. I've been a collector ever since. The visits I made to my relatives on the Orkney Isles filled my curiosity towards the wonders of jewelry—it was such a special place with distinctive jewelry designs. My first collection, 'Percussion' was inspired by my ancestral home in Orkney.

I'm still a keen collector. Now it's of percussion instruments. I realized as soon as my parents bought me my second pair of percussion sticks that I was going to be a collector of something!

I also knew pretty well from the start that I could and would be a professional musician and create a career as the first ever full-time solo percussionist —something unthought of at that time. Belief and determination were paramount, not to mention a good dose of humour.

For all this, the person I still find most inspiring is my dad (he wanted to be a musician but he was the youngest of a very large family, left school at 14 and immediately started to work on his family farm. He found his love for the accordion, taught himself and played Scottish traditional music by ear. I guess he may now be playing his accordion in heaven and I often feel that my playing is for and by, him, his very self.

I still find it useful even now amidst all my current doings, to stop once in a while so I can pull together the strands of my overall vision. Early on, I became convinced of that repeated mantra that has guided me all my life—that you must follow your instincts and believe in yourself even if others don't.

But of course I did believe in myself and in the beautiful art of percussion, and in music's power to bring people together and prevail Suggested change to 'endure'.

Always, I have sought to persevere with that vision—and to succeed. And in doing so to be able, as you will be too, to make a difference in the world.

Photograph © Andy McCreeth

I can say that looking back to my childhood efforts I am proud that the career of the full-time solo percussionist has proved itself to be, without doubt, sustainable. That was my aim from the start. I am also proud that I have discovered new ways of listening, without which I would never have been able to pursue my career.

The best piece of advice I received many years ago was to 'know your stuff' (know what you are doing), know who you are working with and who your audience is and give them your best! Practise the art of creating your own opportunities, take as many opportunities as possible and always believe in yourself.

I could at this point go back and talk in detail about my wonderful growing up on a farm in Scotland, gradually losing my hearing from the age of 8 (the last thing I consciously recall hearing was the throb of a tractor) and learning that the point isn't whether you hear or don't hear but whether you pay attention.

Hearing is a medical condition whereas listening is an act of doing, something that one decides to engage in.

I resisted learning sign language as a child because I felt myself as being aural and I wanted to keep my voice active and controlled) and I was

Photograph © Andy McCreeth

dead set against being sent to a school for the deaf, knowing there was no way there that, at that time, I could go on with my music. Fortunately, my father agreed.

I lived in times whereby people viewed deafness as being about silence—one could hear or not hear—music was about sound so how could silence and sound meet? How could a person living in a world of silence understand and interact with sound? This seemed an impossibility until the advancement of technology and medicine which has allowed us to understand more the complexities of deafness and how it is rarely about silence.

But I won't go on about all that here or about my family background—you can read all of that in my autobiography *Good Vibrations*. I will say, though, that I was very lucky in my parents—without the piano learning and the instruments they gave in to buying me I'm not sure the journey of percussion would ever have happened.

Or maybe it would—my destiny for sure, percussion.

Triangles and eyes—me!

Photograph © Andy McCreeth

Freedom in Percussion

To be a good musician, there must first of all be the seed that comes from the heart, something to grow from.

I remember my first public performance. Ohh! It was when I was only 8 years old and I had been playing the piano for a short but had gained the highest mark in the country for my grade 1 piano exam! I felt so proud up there on the platform—the one in charge. The beginning of so much. Not yet percussion, but yes, the beginning of many performance events and always a great learning experience.

And then—a percussionist! Evelyn Glennie— Concert Solo Percussionist!

One of my fondest memories is of playing the first percussion concerto in the history of the Proms, at the Albert Hall, London in 1992. That truly glorious occasion paved the way for orchestras around the world to feature percussion concertos. It literally changed the landscape of percussion and the audience relationship with it.

And then—the Olympic Opening Ceremony of London 2012, those truly global events. The reception received when performing at events like these are proof that music really does affect all of us, connecting us in ways that the spoken word cannot.

Do you find that incredibly moving?

I was so proud therefore to be a featured solo performer in the opening ceremony of the Deaf

Olympics in Taipei in 2009 and guest performer in the Winter Olympics in Salt Lake City in 2002, then, in July 2012, to have been given a lead role in the London Olympic Opening Ceremony!

Beyond that I've been so lucky to have had the opportunity to collaborate with such a diverse range of artists, not only musicians but dancers, visual artists, theatre, television, radio artists and much more.

Working with the wonderfully creative Björk allowed me to break away from the written page and fall into a completely differentarena, audience-wise.

And then giving totally improvised performances with guitarist Fred Frith is also always an exhilarating experience. We're asking the audience to listen in a completely different way when improvising music on the spot.

Another great percussion experience for me was the innovative brand of performance I was able to develop when working with Hugo Ticciati's String Quartet. They'd been making music together for

'TOUCH THE SOUND' DVD COVER

https://www.evelyn.co.uk/shop/music/dvds/touch-the-sound-dvd/

a number of years, performing at festivals across Europe, combining old and new music in innovative and daring ways, nurturing the sacred ground of the great quartet tradition while challenging its established order, pushing the traditional boundaries of the form and (dare we say) releasing the quartet from the safety of its ivory tower. They are constantly opening up new imaginative spaces, unraveling multiple strands of quartet playing and reweaving them to reveal unforeseen potentialities.

So you see—one of the interesting things is the combination of that raw hand on the instrument and the technology that can transmit it further.

I'm also now a leading commissioner of new works for solo percussion, and by now have more than 200 pieces to my name from many of the world's most eminent composers—crucial for my success as a solo percussionist. In the past there just weren't enough works out there for solo percussion but to my (and audience's) joy, it has built up to such a degree that solo percussion is becoming much more frequent my extempore percussion playing to

their fresh and original musical textures and I can do something to explaining—and demonstrate—extempore for young people who don't know.

The wonders of technology and social media mean we are able to tap into the many projects and collaborations, too long to list here, and explore more how these events have impacted, not only my journey, but those around me too.

My many and ever growing solo recordings, are as diverse as my career.

'Shadow Behind the Iron Sun', 'Sound Spirits' and the Core-Tet Project demonstrate the power of improvisational skills. And then there was the 'Shadow Show'. What an experience of freedom I had in choosing whichever instruments I wanted. One was—yes!—cutting an old mini (car) in half and playing it! (You can see something of our collection of CDs and DVDS at www.evelyn.co.uk)

It's important that I expand the repertoire by continuing to commission and collaborate with a diverse range of composers while recognising the young talent coming through. It all, of course, like

everything else in my life, grew out of my fascination with percussion and sound creation and the desire to make it better known and accessible.

By now I am also recognised as a composer in my own right. I suppose it's partly the result of my GRAMMY awards and BAFTA nomination that I now have a standing that gives me such great opportunities to develop my musical imagination, whether for the concert platform, film, radio, television, theatre or just my own enjoyment...

* * *

My music for the short film about Helen Keller, 'Whirlpool' was very special for me (a taste of this at https://m.youtube.com/watch?v=qMU6wzAaI-A/). Helen is best known for her achievements whilst being deaf and blind, but what people often forget is her ability to hear music with her body. I resonate to that.

In 1924 she wrote an incredibly moving letter to the York Symphony Orchestra about how, listening (deaf) to Beethoven's Ninth Symphony on the radio, explaining how she had been overwhelmed, in a "glorious hour" by its grandeur.

Alright that is not a percussion piece. But there is much in common nevertheless: the journey of sound, 'the vibration", as she puts it, "the impassioned rhythm, the throb and the urge of the music.'

Helen Keller knew by then that blind people could get great joy from music but had not thought that (being deaf) she could share that. However, when the performance came on the radio one of her relations unscrewed a cap on the instrument and encouraged Helen to hold her hand lightly on the sensitive diaphram beneath. She was amazed and enchanted by the intertwining vibrations from the different instruments, which through her touch, she was independently, able to differentiate: timpani, trumpets, violas and violins singing and intermingling, and then the "ecstatic flame-like" human voices, which she recognised instantly. "My heart almost stood still" at this "ocean of heavenly vibration".

Helen was even more moved by the knowledge that, like herself, Beethoven, the great German composer, was already himself deaf when he composed the symphony that untied a nation. She marvelled at the "quenchless spirit by which out of his pain he wrought such joy for others—and there, she goes on, amazed - "I sat, feeling with my hand the magnificent symphony which broke like a sea upon the silen shores of his soul and mine."

She comments on this experience of feeling with

her hand:

"Of course this was not 'hearing', but I do know that the tones and harmonies conveyed to me moods of great beauty and majesty. I also sensed, or thought I did, the tender sounds of nature that sing into my hand-swaying reeds and winds and the murmur of streams. I have never been so enraptured before by a multitude of tone-vibrations"

(The full letter and its history can be read at http://www.lettersofnote.com/2014/03/my-heart-almost-stood-still.html/).

Yes, life is full of challenges, but we can always find alternative ways of approaching our difficulties. And it is this that often leads us to new discoveries.

Coming back to the present I also like "The Invisible Made Audible', a nice title for a percussionist.

Many of the films and media projects that I've been lucky enough to participate in can be found or heard on my website (www.evelyn.co.uk). The film 'Touch the Sound' and my accompanying

Photograph © Andy McCreeth

TED speech will give you a good general idea of my approach to sound and listening (as at https://www.youtube.com/watch?v=Edkx6ovQ9YM/).

* * *

Of course, to put all this in context, you have to remember that innovation and improvisation are nothing new. The history of western classical music is filled with a rich legacy of great improvisers. The list is long and profound: Bach, Mozart, Beethoven, Schubert, Brahms, Franck, Chopin, Liszt, Debussy, Handel and many more. Even before the "jazz" music we now hear everywhere there was the "figured bass" shorthand (1600-1750), which allowed organists and accompanists to perform complex harmonic structures using a common shared numerical language to express specific chords and inversions (the chord the other way up) and in that sense do it their own way.

So each improvised concert is a new and

With Marc Brew's dancers

spontaneous work of art and power—and beauty too—much like the organ works of the baroque period and the great cadenzas of the romantic composer/performers—virtuosic, often improvised passages by a performer within a larger work.

My ventures in that direction have been amazing for me. It's been great to work with the improvising Core-tet group (clever name!) and make a new project together, and to join forces with Joss Arnott Dance. It was incredible to perform live on stage the thundering score that composer James Keane created for the climax of the triple bill "Wide Awakening" with Joss. Then there was the remarkable "Animotion", the brainchild of Russian artist Maria Rud, whose shows push the boundaries of visual art and music installation, blending real-time painting, live musical performance and projection mapping.

The result is a feast for the senses as live music enriches the soundscape in complete synchrony with the visual transformations.

Another extraordinary setting for my percussion

With Peter Eustance in the sound garden

playing and experience of sound was conceived by choreographer Marc Brew in partnership with DanceEast, and the highly evocative score co-composed by myself and Philip Sheppard. "Fusional Fragments" explored the concept of fusing life fragments between classical ballet and contemporary dance, a breathtaking departure from the norm, as my highly gestural performance style—frequently described as a vivid dance-like experience in itself—became integrated into the onstage action.

I remember too the time we broke new ground at the Edinburgh International Science Festival with the world premiere of the "Sounds of Science" (www.youtube.com/watch?v=HlaPGvkUG9I/). This was an audio-narration that took its audience on a unique interactive journey through a timeline of science, from the stone ages to the present day, showing how humans have changed the world—from the first stone tools through to discovery of Newton's laws of motion and gravity, the nuclear age and beyond.

Vanuatu from the air

All this was using nothing more than—just sound.

And gardening too. Did you know that music and gardening—well, anything—can be related? Disability and music too.

Yes, inspired by my percussion playing, Peter Eustance of Symphonic Gardens developed an acoustic Artisan Garden for the disability charity, Papworth Trust called the "Together We Can Garden".

They built an acoustic pulse inspired by the 'sea music' produced by the women of the remote Pacific islands of Vanuatu who create amazing rhythmic songs with just their hands, water and voices.

And then just think how important clapping has been in the history of music. Clapping and stomping are often essential for the rhythms and actions of music and dance: the primary percussion modes, aren't they, our bodies.

Beyond such public performances, collaborations and compositions, I especially love question-and-answer sessions with young people such as

yourselves. Master-classes that bring me into personal contact with young musicians and give me the chance to learn something from them are very valuable. It's a very special exchange.

My live webinar with primary school teachers and trainee teachers was another way of celebrating the learning potential of sound-discovery and music-making. The session was devised and run by Webinology and involved schools and universities from across the globe, an opportunity for me to further my commitment to music in education. I am convinced that one of the most important ways to stimulate high quality learning is to equip our teachers with the tools, knowledge and inspiration to build an unforgettable learning experience.

Such a list! But then I do give many performances a year worldwide, performing with the world's greatest conductors, orchestras, and artists and these are just a few I have listed.

Hopefully these are enough to show the amazing versatility of percussion and how it is magically amazing and liberating. Liberated sounds both speak for themselves and in turn enrich and liberate us too.

There is never an end to creativity in music and its playing or to percussion's potential for imaginative, improvised vision and breaking new boundaries.

There is never an end to creativity in music and its playing or to percussion's potential for imaginative, improvised vision and breaking new boundaries.

The vibrating hearing body

Listening is the backbone to every aspect of our lives.

Music represents life.

Yes truly. A particular piece of music may represent—describe—a real, fictional or abstract scene from almost any area of human experience or imagination. It is the musician's job to paint a picture which communicates the scene the composer is trying to describe to the audience.

So I always hope that my listeners will be stimulated by what I have to say (throug the language of music) and leave the concert hall feeling entertained. If the audience is instead only wondering how a deaf musician can play percussion then I have failed as a musician.

For this reason, my deafness is not mentioned in any of the information supplied by my office to the press or concert promoters.

Unfortunately, however, my deafness makes good headlines. Ugh! I have learnt from childhood that if I refuse to discuss my deafness with the media, they will just make it up. The several hundred articles and reviews written about me every year add up to a total of many thousands and only a handful of them accurately describe my hearing impairment. More than 90% are so inaccurate that you would be forgiven for thinking that it is impossible for me to be a musician.

So this chapter is designed to set the record straight and allow you to enjoy the experience of being entertained by an ever evolving, learning, experimenting musician rather than some freak or miracle of nature.

Deafness is, in general, poorly understood.

For instance, there is a common misconception that deaf people live in a world of silence. But to understand the nature of deafness, first one has to understand the nature of hearing.

Hearing is basically a specialized form of touch. Yes, touch. It's a bit hard to describe touch exactly, and how it reaches you, but in essence, sound-touch is simply vibrating air. You feel it don't you! It is this that the ear picks up and converts to electrical signals and these are then interpreted by the brain.

But the sense of (ear) hearing is not the only sense that can do this. As I say, (and as you know already) touch can do it too.

Take this example. You are standing by the road and a large truck goes by. Do you hear or feel the vibration? The answer is both. With very low frequency vibration the ear starts becoming inefficient and the rest of the body's sense of touch starts to take over. For some reason we tend to make a distinction between hearing a sound and feeling a vibration, in reality they are the same thing.

It is interesting to note that in the Italian language this distinction does not exist. The verb 'sentire' means to hear and the same verb in another form 'sentirsi' means to feel.

Deafness does not mean that you can't hear, only that there is something wrong with the ears. Even someone who is totally deaf can still hear/feel sounds.

If we can all feel low frequency vibrations why can't we feel higher vibrations? It is my belief that we can, it's just that as the frequency gets higher and our ears become more efficient they drown out the more subtle sense of 'feeling' the vibrations.

I spent a lot of time in my youth (with the help of my school percussion teacher Ron Forbes) refining my ability to detect vibrations. I would stand with my hands against the classroom wall while Mr Forbes played pitches on the timpani (these drums produce a lot of vibrations).

Eventually I managed to distinguish the rough pitch of notes by associating where on my body I felt the sound with the sense of perfect pitch I had before losing my hearing. The low sounds I feel mainly in my legs and feet (I often play barefoot) and high sounds might be particular places on my face, neck, chest and scalp.

It is worth pointing out at this stage that I am not totally deaf, I am *profoundly* deaf, which is different. Profound deafness covers a wide range of symptoms, although it is commonly taken to mean that the quality of the sound heard is not sufficient to be able to understand the spoken word from sound alone. With no other sound interfering, I can usually hear someone speaking, although I cannot understand them without the additional input of lip-reading.

In my case, the amount of volume is reduced compared with normal hearing but more importantly, the quality of the sound is very poor. For instance when a phone rings I hear a kind of crackle. However, it is a distinctive type of crackle that I associate with a phone so I know when the phone rings.

This is basically the same as how normally

Photograph © Andy McCreeth

hearing people detect a phone, it has a distinctive type of ring which we associate with a phone. I can in fact communicate over the phone. I do most of the talking whilst the other person can say a few words by striking the transmitter with a pen, I hear this as clicks. I have a code that depends on the number of strikes or the rhythm that I can use to communicate a handful of words.

So far we've talked of the hearing of sounds and the feeling of vibrations.

There is one other element to the equation. This (you've guessed it) is sight.

We can see items move and vibrate. If I see a drum head or cymbal vibrate or even see the leaves of a tree moving in the wind then subconsciously my brain creates a corresponding sound.

We all inhabit a resonating body, each of us differently.

We have our own sound, our own way of hearing and creating. A common question from interviewers is 'How can you be a musician when you can't hear what you are doing?' The answer is,

Photograph © Andy McCreeth

of course, that I couldn't be a musician if I were not able, in my own way, to hear.

Another often asked question is 'How do you hear what you are playing?' The logical answer to this is 'How does anyone hear?' An electrical signal is generated in the ear and various bits of other information from our other senses all get sent to the brain which then processes the data to create a sound picture.

The various processes involved in hearing a sound are very complex, but we all do it subconsciously, we group all these processes together and call it simply "hearing".

The same is true for me. Some of the processes or original information may be different but to hear sound all I do is to listen. I have no more idea of how I hear than you do.

For me, as for all of us, I am better at certain things with my hearing than others. I need to lip-read to understand speech but my awareness of the acoustics in a concert venue is excellent. For instance, I will sometimes describe an acoustic in terms of how thick the air feels.

You will notice that these answers are heading more towards areas of philosophy. Who can say that when two normally hearing people hear a sound they hear the same sound? I would suggest that everyone's hearing is different. All we can say is that the sound-picture built up by their brain is the same, so that outwardly there is no difference.

To summarize, my hearing is something that bothers other people far more than it bothers me. In fact, rather than isolating me it gives me an extra connection with my music. It's true that there are a couple of inconveniences but in general it doesn't affect my life much. For me, my deafness is no more important than the fact I am female with brown eyes. Yes, I sometimes have to find solutions to problems regarding my hearing and its relationship to music, but so do all musicians.

Most of us know very little about hearing, even though we do it all the time.

Likewise, I don't know very much about deafness. What's more, I'm not particularly interested. I remember one occasion when, uncharacteristically, I became upset with a reporter for constantly asking questions only about my deafness. I said 'If you want to know about deafness, you should interview an audiologist. My specialism is music'.

So, please, just enjoy the music and forget the rest.

Photograph © Andy McCreeth

To feel, to connect,
to truly listen

My aim is To Teach the World to Listen.

Yes, my job is all about listening and teaching others to listen. That's my real aim in life.

My vision is a society where communication and social cohesion are improved by the act of listening. I want, as I like to put it, to 'Teach the World to Listen' through profound musical, educational and charitable/social experiences, that is, to use the tools of performance, advocacy, consultancy and education to inspire active, receptive listening, both to ourselves and others.

Snare drums

And who am I thinking of?

Everyone. Our work is for people today and for future generations, locally and internationally.

That maybe sounds very simple, but actually, it's quite a big job.

When you look at piece of notated music, for example, it is full of little black dots on the page and we say we 'read the music'.

Well technically, I *can* read what's on the piece of paper. I can see those little dots. I can follow the instructions, the tempo markings, the dynamics. I'll do exactly as I'm told.

So—I play it.

That's straightforward; there's nothing too difficult about that. I'm being told that this piece of music is very quick. I'm being told where to play on the drum. I'm being told which part of the stick to use. And I'm being told the dynamic.

And I'm also being told that the drum is without snares (the stiff wires held under tension against the lower skin that produce a rattling sound). Snares on, snares off.

So therefore, if I translate this piece of music, we have a series of drum sounds (you can hear these sounds - please do, that's the point after all - and my voice as well if you want it, on the video at https://www.ted.com/talks/evelyn_glennie_shows_how_to_listen/).

But what I have to do *as a musician* is do everything that is *not* on the written page; everything that often there isn't time to learn or to discuss with a teacher It's the things you notice when you're not actually with your instrument that become so interesting, that you then want to explore through this tiny, tiny surface of a drum.

So first, we experienced the translation. Now we need to experience the interpretation (for these drum sounds, and the following examples, again listen to the video).

In a way, you know, it's the same process as if I look at you and I see, say, a nice, bright young lady with a pink top on. I see that you're clutching a scarf. I get a basic idea as to what you might be about, what you might like, what you might do as a profession, and so on. However, that's just the initial idea I may have, the kind that we all get when we actually look and try to interpret. But actually, it's so unbelievably shallow.

In the same way, I look at the music; I get a basic idea; I wonder what might be hard technically, or what I want to do to explore the basic landscape of a piece.

But that's simply not enough. And please—listen, listen, listen!

We have to listen to ourselves, first of all. If you play, for example, by holding the stick really tightly—you'll feel quite a lot of shock coming up through the arm when striking the drum. And believe it or not—detached from the instrument and from the stick, even though you're actually holding that stick quite tightly. Yes it's true, in holding it tightly, I feel strangely more detached.

If I just simply let go and allow my hand, my arm, to be more of a support system, suddenly—listen! More dynamic, less effort! More freedom, more choices. Dynamics are produced both horizontally and vertically—high and fat, low and shallow. I just feel, at last, one with the stick an one with the drum. And I'm using far less energy.

So in the same way that I need time with this instrument, I need time with people in order to interpret them. Not just translate them, but *interpret* them. There is a bit of a difference there that is worth just thinking about.

I remember when I was 12 years old, and I started playing timpani and percussion, my teacher said,

"Well, how are we going to do this? You know, music is about listening".

"Yes," I said, "I agree with that, so what's the problem?"

"Well, how are you going to hear this? How are you going to hear that?"

"Well, how do *you* hear it?" I asked

"Well," pointing to his ears, "I think I hear it through here."

I said,

"Well, I think I do too, but I also hear it through my hands, through my arms, cheekbones, my scalp, my tummy, my chest, my legs and so on."

And so we began our lessons every single time by

tuning the drums, in particular the kettle drums or timpani, to a narrow pitch interval, beginning large then narrower and narrower (listen inner ear!—or whatever). And it's amazing that when you do open your body up, and open your hand up to allow the vibration to come through, that in fact the tiny, tiny tiniest difference can be felt with just the tiniest part of your finger as you lightly touch it.

And so what we would do is that I would put my hands on the wall of the music room, and, together, we would "listen" to the sounds of the instruments, and really try to connect with those sounds far, far more broadly than simply depending on the ear.

Because of course, the ear is subject to all sorts of things. The room we happen to be in, the amplification, the quality of the instrument, the type of sticks etc., etc., they're all different. Maybe they'll have the same amount of weight, say, but different sound colours, and so on.

And that's basically what we are; we're just human beings, but we all have our own little sound colours, as it were, that make up these extraordinary personalities and characters and interests and things.

At the age of 16, I auditioned for the Royal Academy of Music in London, and they said,

"Well, no, we can't accept you, because we haven't a clue, you know, of the future of a so-called 'deaf musician'."

I just couldn't accept that.

And so I said to them, "Well, look, if you refuse—if you refuse me for those reasons, as opposed to the ability to perform and to understand and love the art of creating sound—then we have to think very, very hard about the people you do actually accept."

And as a result, once we got over a little bit of a hurdle, and having to audition twice, they accepted me. And not only that, what had happened was—this is so great—that it changed the whole role of the music institutions throughout the United Kingdom.

Under no circumstances are they now going to refuse any application whatsoever on the basis of whether someone has a disability. For example, if someone has no arms, no legs, they could still, say, play a wind instrument if it was supported on a stand. No irrelevant circumstances at all are used to refuse entry. And every single entry has to be listened to and experienced. Then, based on musical ability alone, that person is either accepted or not.

And this in turn, means that there is an extremely interesting group of students going through these various music institutions now, and many of them with hugely successful careers ahead of them. Quite simply, that not only are people connected with sound, which is basically all of us—we recognise that music really is our daily medicine.

I say "music," but actually I mean "sound", the journey of the sound. There are some extraordinary things I've experienced as a musician. I remember a young man who had many physical and mental challenges who was not able to control his movements. He was placed underneath the marimba, lying on his back.

Suddenly, as I played, this boy became so still and peaceful to the point that it even amazed his

In the sounds of waves.

Support Workers and teachers. The difference in his being from when sitting in the auditorium to being under the marimba absorbing the vibration across his whole body was astounding. From underneath, he was one with the instrument—an extension to the marimba.

He would have a fullness of sound that people sitting in the front few rows at a performance wouldn't experience, those in the back few rows wouldn't experience, either. Every single one of us, depending on where we're sitting, will experience this quite quite differently.

The interesting thing about this as well is quite simply that not only are people connected with sound—which is basically all of us—we recognise well now that music really *is* our daily medicine.

Sound is always there, part of the universe. All around us whether we consciously listen to it or not.

Here and now for example you might think you see me touching the instrument, and so expect to hear the sound in your head and indeed you think you do hear sound but actually—you hear nothing

In the rhythms of a horse's thudding hooves.

In the vibrations of music.

because I'm not actually touching the instrument. Even so, you get the sensation of something happening.

In the same way that when I see a tree move, then I imagine that tree making a rustling sound. Do you see what I mean? Whatever the eye sees, then there's always sound happening. So there's always, always this huge—I mean, just this kaleidoscope of things to draw from.

So all of my performances are based entirely on what I experience. It's not by learning a piece of music, putting on someone else's interpretation of it, buying all the CDs possible of that particular piece of music, and so on and so forth, because that wouldn't give me enough of something that is so raw and so basic, something that I can fully experience the journey of.

So it may be that, in certain halls, a really soft dynamic may work well. But in other halls, the listeners are simply not going to experience it at all, and so therefore, my level of soft, gentle playing may have to be greatly increased.

In our breathing and in the beating of our hearts.

Do you see what I mean, my readers, listeners?

The explosion of increased access to sound nowadays, notably throughout the deaf community, due to advancements in technology such as cochlear implants or detecting deafness as early as when the baby is still in the mother's womb has affected how music institutions, how schools for the deaf treat sound, and not just as a means of therapy. Although, that is important too.

It has also meant that acousticians have had to really think about the types of halls they put together. There are so few halls in this world that actually have very good acoustics, dare I say. By that I mean, where you can absolutely do anything you could imagine. Good acoustics have the effect of throwing the tiniest, softest, softest sound to something that is so broad, so huge, so incredible. There's always something a challenge: it may sound good up there, may not be so good there; it may be great there, but terrible up there; maybe terrible over there, but not too bad there and so on...

So to find an actual good hall is amazing...one in which you can play exactly what you imagine, without it being cosmetically enhanced. Therefore, acousticians are sometimes in conversation with people who are hearing-impaired, and who are participants of sound because hearing-impaired people, like myself, relate to sound through our whole body, not just our ears, far as what is actually happening with those halls, but it's just the fact that they are now taking accounts of a group of people's real experience.

"Well, how on earth can they experience music? No way. They're deaf! Ignore".

We assume this and imagine that's what deafness is about. Nothing! Silence!

We think the same about blindness. Empty! Blackness! If we see someone in a wheel chair, we assume they cannot walk. It may be that they can walk three, four, five steps. That, to them, means they can walk. In a year's time, it could be two extra steps. In another year's time, three extra steps.

These are hugely important aspects to think

about.

So when we do listen to each other, it's unbelievably important for us to really test our listening skills, to really use our bodies as a resonating chamber, to stop the uninformed judging and assumptions.

For me, as a musician who deals with 99 percent of new music, it's very easy for me to say,

"Oh yes, I like that piece" or "No, I don't like that piece," and so on.

I just find that I have to give those pieces of music real time. It may be that the chemistry isn't quite right between myself and that particular piece of music, but that doesn't mean I have the right to say it's a bad piece of music. And you know, one of the great things about being a musician is that it is so unbelievably fluid.

So there are no rules, no right, no wrong this way, that way.

If I asked you (even now while you are peacefully reading this, maybe at home perhaps at school or college to clap...yes maybe I can do this. I can just say:

"Please clap and create the sound of thunder."

I'm assuming we've all experienced thunder. Now, I don't mean just the sound; I mean really feel and listen to that thunder within yourself. And try to create that through clapping.

Try, just—please try.

Now—try *snow*.

Yes. Snow.

Well, have you ever heard snow? No? Well, then (laugh) stop clapping! Try again.

Yes. Silence, isn't that right? Yes silence.

Now—rain. Rain on a roof-top, rain on leaves, rain on cobbles, rain on your raincoat.

Yes, that's right, vary your clapping depending on the rain of your imagination.

Yes, that's right, light clapping sounds, quite right, you heard it pattering down.

Thank you.

But the interesting thing, though, is that when I did this with an audience, not one of them got out of their seats to think, "Right! How can I clap? OK, maybe on the ground, *thump, thump*, on a different part if my body, my head my cheeks, whatever... Maybe use their jewelry to create extra sounds. Maybe other parts of their body again to create extra sounds for the thunder noise. Not a single person thought about clapping in a different way opfrom just sitting there in their seats there and using two hands.

In the same way, when we listen to music, we assume that it's all being fed through the ears, that this is how we experience music.

Of course, it's not.

For example—we experience thunder... Thunder, *thunder.*

Think, think, think.
Listen, listen, listen.

What can we do with thunder? I remember my teacher, when I first started, my very first lesson, I was all prepared with sticks, ready to go. And instead of him saying what I expected, like,

"Okay, Evelyn, please, feet slightly apart, arms at a more or less 90-degree angle, sticks in a more or less V shape, keep this amount of space here, etc. Please keep your back straight, etc., etc., etc."—

And I would probably just have ended up absolutely rigid, frozen, and not be able to strike the drum at all because I was having to think of so many other things. But he simply said,

"Evelyn, take this drum away for seven days, no sticks and I'll see you next week."

So—heavens! What was I to do? I wasn't even allowed to have the sticks. So I just had to basically look at this particular drum, see how it was made, what these little lugs did, what the snares did. Turned it upside down, experimented with the shell? how did that sound?

Experimented with the head. What about that?

Experimented with my body and the drum. Aha...

Experimented with my jewelry on the drum.

Experimented putting the drum on a cushion, on grass, on cement, on straw.

Each surface made the drum resonate and therefore 'speak' differently.

All those sounds from that one drum!

And of course (you'll laugh), I went back with all sorts of bruises.

All the same, it was such an unbelievable experience, because where on earth are you going to experience that in a notated piece of music? Where on earth are you going to experience that in a study book? So we never, ever dealt with actual study books. We always dealt with pieces of music and improvisation.

And interestingly, the older I became, and when I became a full-time student at a so-called "music institution," all of that went out of the window. We had to study from study books. And constantly, the question,

"Well, why? Why? What is this relating to? I need to play a piece of music."

"Well, this will help your control."

"Well, *how*?' I would question, "Why do I need to learn that in isolation? I need to relate it to a piece of music. I tell you, I need to *say* something with my *music*. So why am I practicing paradiddles? is it just literally for control, for hand-stick control? Why am I doing that? I need to have the reason, and the reason has to be by saying something through the *music*."

By saying something through music, which basically is sound, we then can reach all sorts of emotions to all sorts of people.

I can't take responsibility for *your* emotional baggage, that's up to you, when you walk into a hall, that's what determines how *you* listen to certain things. I may feel sorrowful, or happy, or exhilarated, or angry when I play certain pieces of music, but I'm not necessarily wanting you to feel exactly the same thing.

So please, the next time you go to a concert, just allow your body to open up, allow your body to be this resonating chamber. Be aware that you're not always going to experience the same thing as the performer is. You have permission to feel what you wish!

In fact—you may not realise this—the performer is in the worst possible position for experiencing the actual sound because they're hearing the contact of the stick on the drum, or the mallet on the bit of wood, or the bow on the string, etc… or the breath that's creating the sound from wind and brass. They're experiencing that rawness of attack.

But still, they're experiencing something so unbelievably pure, before the sound actually happening. So take note of the life of the sound after the actual initial strike, or breath, is being pulled. Listen to the resonance and how the room or space you are in becomes the instrument, not what you see on stage.

I hope we can share all this and more as we travel the ways of and experience the wonders if sound together.

Photograph © Andy McCreeth

The ring of words, the sound of music

"The isle is full of noises, sounds and sweet airs, that give delight and hurt not."

As I thumb through the works of William Shakespeare, I find myself feeling sounds, a subject close to my heart. I learnt to use my body to feel music when I began to lose my hearing as a child. When I reached *The Tempest*, the words positively shouted sound to me—even the title has a strong resonance. The island of Shakespeare's *The*

Tempest is physical and responsive, and "full of sounds".

Here Prospero, the rightful Duke of Milan, speaks:

"To cry to th' sea that roar'd to us; to sigh
To th' winds, whose pity, sighing back again,
Did us but loving wrong."

The language here takes me back to my homeland. I lived on a farm at the top of a hill in Aberdeenshire, where a walk on the cliffs forces me to face the winds, and I can feel the sound on my cheeks. When recounting the story of how Prospero and his daughter Miranda came to be on the island, Miranda reminds us about the feeling of sound we get when we cry:

"I, not rememb'ring how I cried out then,
Will cry it o'er again; it is a hint
That wrings mine eyes to't."

I can still feel the sting of the tears as the North Sea wind catches my eyes, for when I was upset, tears would trickle down my cheeks, and I would feel them slowly descending towards my lips.

I wonder if Shakespeare knew what I have discovered and shared?

That the whole body can hear.

Reading his work, I could almost feel the sound of the pen scratching at the paper—etching out the narrative in such a way, sound becomes paramount to the play. Each character echoes sound, and Shakespeare entices us into their tales, using sound to colour their characters.

For me sound is about depth of feeling. I have found a way to substitute for my hearing loss. I immerse myself into the senses within my skin, bones and muscles. I discovered a whole new set of hearing tools through ambient vibration.

Shakespeare's *The Tempest* plays to my sensory world. He uses sound to describe emotions:

humour / pride / anguish / shame / authority and subservience—throughout the tale. For example, Antonio, who we are told usurped his brother's position, shouts at the sailors, 'Hang, cur! Hang, you whoreson insolent noise-maker!' I am tempted to replicate the emotions' meanings through my percussion instruments!

The use of sound colours what we most enjoy as the play unfolds. I wonder if actors relish the opportunities to express themselves through the sounds of the characters? I have spent most of my life encouraging people to engage in a richer world of sound, by tuning into the 'pretence' of silence.

It is my belief there is no such thing as silence. To experience this we need to turn off all surrounding sound and contemplate the remaining chasm, which should be silence. You will discover thus another sound world, where you can truly begin to understand how to tap into a different way of listening. By putting your hand on your chest, you can feel your own beating heart.

I have learnt to interpret those feelings

throughout my body. Shakespeare slows the tempo down as he brings the gentle Miranda and Ariel to us. Miranda makes the profound statement to her father, 'Your tale, sir, would cure deafness.' Now I am really hooked!

One of the reasons sound is so central to *The Tempest* is tightly bound up with the fate of Ariel, an airy spirit, who is earning his freedom from Prospero by performing great feats for his master. The play opens with the great storm Ariel has raised, and the consequent shipwreck brings to the island Prospero's ancient enemy, his brother Antonio. In order to realise his schemes, Prospero requires Ariel to become invisible:

"Go make thyself like a nymph o'th' sea. Be subject To no sight but thine and mine, invisible."

The only trace of the invisible is the sounds they make. That's why sound is centre stage in *The Tempest*, and in his invisible state, Ariel sings and plays his song full of earthly sounds:

ARIEL: *Come unto these yellow sands,*
And then take hands.
Curtsied when you have, and kissed.
The wild waves whist.
Foot it featly here and there,
And sweet sprites bear
The burden.
SPIRITS: *Hark, hark! Bow-wow!*

I imagine a twinkle or glint as Ariel flits from pillar to post, weaving in and out of the players, singing his song, while Ferdinand, son of Alonso, the King of Naples, asks, 'Where should this music be? I' th' air or th'earth?'

I like the idea of music being around and within us. I have spent my life learning to experience sound to enable my body to transfer the impact of the feelings I get from sounds, which most hear via the ears, to my brain.

How can I deny Shakespeare intended us to read the most musical sounds into his play when he presents us with the second verse of Ariel's song? I reach for yet another bell to accompany his words!

"Hark, hark. I hear
The strain of strutting Chanticleer
Cry, cock-a-diddle-dow."

The Tempest is a vibrant mix of many sounds of land and sea and wind and surf. Rhythm is present throughout the text and lyrics. Passion is deeply embedded within the emotions.

I am perhaps more sensitive to the passion and emotion of sounds because of my hearing loss. I have had to learn what each sound represents, rather than taking them for granted. My whole body is similar to an ear, every surface has learnt to become a conduit, bringing meaning and sense to my brain. Whereas Shakespeare crafts his words, I sense he is wanting his audiences to experience them in their completeness. He uses his wordcraft to immerse and engage us, as if we were actually participating in the play.

Every phrase resounds,

'SPIRITS: *Ding dong.*
ARIEL: *Hark, now I hear them.*
SPIRITS: *Ding dong, bell.*'

My own senses are jumping between the emotional words of Ferdinand as he fears the loss of his father. Perplexed, he listens to Ariel,

"... nor no sound
That the earth owes. I hear it now above me."

Shakespeare leaves us to imagine the horrific sounds of the storm that left King Alonso, Sebastian, Antonio, Gonzalo, Adrian, Francisco and members of the crew stranded on another part of the island.

For me there is a space to imagine instruments I might select to recreate the sound of the waves crashing onto the wooden decks of the predestined shipwreck. I feel the creaking of the wood as it breaks on the rocks, slapped by the canvas sails splitting the rigging. I ponder, and reach for a mallet; I grasp the wood firmly. As I embrace the scene, it is the same as when I raise my arm to strike the bar. As soon as my arm falls, it is that moment the waves begin to crash onto the rocks—that place of no return. The mallet will strike and the waves will crash.

Amidst the cries of lost souls tossed to a watery grave, I steel myself to introduce the complex sounds from water. I think about creating the sounds of splashing water surfaces, frothing crests and, perhaps, thrusts of water pulling and pushing sand across the beach. Francisco tells the distraught Alonso that he saw his son Fernando:

"...beat the surges under him
And ride upon their backs. He trod the water
Whose enmity he flung aside, and breasted
The surge, most swol'n, that met him. His bold head
'Bove the contentious waves he kept, and oared
Himself with his good arms in lusty stroke
To th' shore, that o'er his wave-worn basis bowed,
As stooping to relieve him. ..."

I consider the rhythm of Fernando's arms thrashing, time and time again, against the water that threatens to drag him down to depths, ending only when the pressure of the water exhausts his final breath. I am reminded of the way a frantic musical performance comes to an end: I catch my breath and bow. But Shakespeare wants not for glory, in this scene he is asking us to experience loss. The waves are deadened and quiet and have left their trail of destruction, lifeless on the beach, with only the swishing hand of the ebb and flow to cover their shame.

As I approach the plotting of Antonio and Sebastian (the brother to Alonso), in which they agree to kill the king so that Sebastian can take up the throne, I feel the breath of whispers in the night:

"... Here lies your brother,
No better than the earth he lies upon
If he were that which now he's like—that's dead—
Whom I with this obedient steel, three inches of it,
Can lay to bed forever; ..."

The weighty silence of conspiracy pounds upon my chest cavity, until Ariel sings a warning into the ear of Prospero's friend Gonzalo:

'While you here do snoring lie,
Open-eyed conspiracy His time doth take.
If of life you keep a care,
Shake off slumber and beware.
Awake, awake!'

The tension in my body rises, as Gonzalo stirs to find a sword drawn above Alonso. Those bleary moments are screaming out to me to escape and run, heart pounding. But no, Shakespeare is a master of wordcraft, and amidst the evil atmosphere in split seconds, his faithful servant Gonzalo speaks: 'Now, good angels preserve the King.' And the startled King responds:

Why, how now? Ho! Awake! [The others awake]… [to Antonio and Sebastian], *'Why are you drawn?'…*

[to Gonzalo], *'Wherefore this ghastly looking?'*

In those few words I feel the sound of a sword being dragged from its sheath, a sharp sound against the dead night, the air heavy with intent and surprise. Oh what magnificent sounds I should create to feel that sinister look upon Sebastian's face as the King wakes from his slumber, and Sebastian's evil intent is thwarted!

The stage directions introducing Caliban combine images of servitude with the sounds of tempests. His plight reminds me of the way we are hostage to sounds. We cannot rest our ears, therefore we must find ways to escape overloading them. My heart goes out to Caliban as he describes his lot, and I feel sounds ooze from the very bellows of the bog that entraps him:

"[A noise of thunder heard].
[Prospero's] *spirits hear me,*
And yet I needs must curse…
Sometime like apes that mow and chatter at me

And after bite me; then like hedgehogs, which
Lie tumbling in my barefoot way and mount
Their pricks at my footfall; sometime am I
All wound with adders, who with cloven tongues
Do hiss me into madness."

Apes' chattering teeth, hedgehogs' pricks, and adders' fangs: I trawl my arsenal of percussion to find something to create these sounds. I want to offer a sound sense of his miserable existence, and to try and bring him a cheerful note. Perhaps Trinculo the jester can do that for me?

Shakespeare interrupts Caliban's complaints about his enslavement with the jolly sea shanty of Stephano, the drunken butler.

Music has the ability to lift the spirits, and Shakespeare utilises its benefits to transform the atmosphere, the warm sound of the small accordion suddenly lifting the mood. I identify especially with Ariel, as (like him) I try to use sound to make something invisible, visible. Caliban's response to music is one of Shakespeare's most famous speeches:

'Be not afeard: the isle is full of noises,
Sounds and sweet airs that give delight and hurt
not.
Sometimes a thousand twangling instruments
Will hum about mine ears; and sometimes voices,
That, if I then had waked after long sleep,
Will make me sleep again; and then, in dreaming,
The clouds methought would open and show riches
Ready to drop upon me, that when I waked
I cried to dream again.'

I am propelled back to the 2012 London Olympics, where these immortal lines were performed. As I prepared for my own performance there, caught up with the moment, I felt separate but not alone.

Later, the thought of the audience, both local and global, was brought home to me when I watched the ceremony on television. Through it all though, I held Caliban's direction 'Be not afeard' close to me—an affirmation of my own mission: to help others develop their own understanding of sound and listening.

As a performer I have always searched for ways to create emotion; each time I lift my arm, I am pulling emotion from the chord up through the body, and releasing it as I begin the approach to the next strike. When I perform 'A Little Prayer', which I wrote as a child, I communicate the deepest emotions by the striking of percussion keys.

The opening bars of 'A little prayer' which I composed for marimba when I was 13, now published as the first of 'Three Chorales' by Faber Music.

Shakespeare's medium is words, but his words simultaneously evoke sounds, and they communicate the most powerful emotions. The 2012 Olympic opening ceremony provided the greatest stage, and I like to imagine Shakespeare turning in his deadly slumber as his words echoed and reached millions around the world. The final lines of *The Tempest*, spoken by Prospero, signal the happy succession of the tempestuous with the calm:

> '...*Now I want*
> *Spirits to enforce, art to enchant;*
> *And my ending is despair,*
> *Unless I be relieved by prayer,*
> *Which pierces so that it assaults Mercy itself and*
> *frees all faults.*
> *As you from crimes would pardoned be,*
> *Let your indulgence set me free.*'

Possibly the last words written by Shakespeare. He requests that his sails are filled and he is released. *The Tempest* has waned, emotions are calm, and forgiveness abounds. He takes a bow and leaves the stage. It has been 400 years and his words are still spoken and recognised around the world.

It is clear to me Shakespeare wrote from his heart, and he brought about honour, pride and awe to his audiences. I admire his spirit and feel I know him through his works.

Hope you do too!

Photograph © Andy McCreeth

What makes us human?

For all the immense achievements of mankind I cannot help but think that a definitive answer to the question 'What makes us human?' eludes us. There is no concise thing we can point to, no simple 'this' or 'that', without more questions being raised. The whole matter is so enormous that it ties my brain in knots! Perhaps the fact that I am able to think about the question at all is what makes me human. In the words of Descartes: *cogito ergo sum*—I think therefore I am.

As a species we continually explore the complexities of our own neurology and the mechanics of our human bodies. We learn more every day about the amazing and surprising ways we exist under both favourable and adverse conditions. For instance, we are coming to realizing that our senses constitute many layers of sub-senses, as I can personally testify.

Human life, as a biological and a social phenomenon, is a difficult subject to tackle all in one go, not least because our individuality is a big part of who we are. There are few traits that everybody exhibits, few parameters that we can use to define all human beings equally and universally.

Recently I have been starkly reminded of the extremes humanity can reach; from the horrors of the wars throughout territories of the world to child trafficking to modern day slavery.

Finding an answer to the question 'what makes us human?' seems particularly hard when viewed in the context of humanity's extreme behaviour.

On a global level I am aware that large groups of people are traumatised by the atrocities of others. In some territories, the use of force and oppression

LISTEN WORLD!

appears to be the favoured method of resolving conflict. Such 'resolution by force' requires somebody—a government, a military body, a judicial system, individuals or whoever—to justify that use of force.

What does this say about us a humans? Clearly some people abuse the system, judging and acting in a way that deprives affected people of their influence, their ability to defend themselves and sometimes their basic human rights. Such control comes in many guises, justified in the name of anything from democracy to dictatorial power.

On the other hand we do often turn to debate in order to resolve our differences. We can debate anything from deciding what to have for lunch to deliberations over major international crises. For example, world leaders at the G8 attempt to find solutions to global problems such as starvation, the lack basic infrastructure for millions of people (in places like Africa) and the vast number of resources wasted elsewhere in the world.

Our ability to debate these topics says something

about our humanity, too, but so does the fact that we allow such terrible things to happen in the first place, not to mention our expectation that there will always be someone else around to solve the problems we create.

I ask myself, therefore, if the answer to my question 'what makes us human?' is compassion. Our capacity for substantial levels of compassion is perhaps easiest to see in the charity sector where people work tirelessly to fund improvement, offer hope and provide mechanisms to end all manner of misery, all for the benefit of others.

Perhaps prayer is the answer; our long legacy of turning to omnipresent, super-human beings to guide us to resolutions we cannot find ourselves and to provide us with spiritual sanctuary from our suffering. Or maybe it is patience that defines us. After all, this is the trait I find myself turning to extremely frequently, whether I am waiting in queues at airports or striving to perfect a piece of music.

Perhaps the answer is simpler than that. I am

human and I have feelings. Do my feelings make me human? If they are I face a conundrum. I know from personal experience that other species such as cats and dogs clearly have feelings too. Having empathy and sensitivity towards others is essential and can make a huge difference to our perception and treatment of others. Such traits are most notably evident in hospitals, hospices and other such caring environments. But there are issues with some organisations, individual care homes and hospitals, where there appears to be a lack of empathy and sensitivity with devastating effect.

Curiosity also plays a large part in what defines us as human. Our curiosity has been directed inward as much as outward. Research into the development and working of the human body has grown to a discipline of unimaginable scale. With every discovery about our humanity we are faced with the question of whether or not we should revise the way we envisage ourselves as human beings. The science of modern medicine has allowed us to overcome challenges that would once have killed us or left us permanently disabled. We have developed cures and prosthetics, we are able to regenerate cells from living tissue and perform countless other procedures that bring, not just the prospect of recovery, but also hope and continued quality of life. Some medical advances raise moral questions, too. For instance, our ability to manipulate human embryos brings joy to families the world over while also raising concerns about the ethical implications of our actions.

This very human sense of curiosity is my mainstay. I have found ways to feel and sense sound that do not rely on the usual physiological methods. My innate curiosity led to the discovery that I could use my body as a resonating chamber and sense sound using the whole of myself rather than only using my ears. I was then able to fulfil my hopes and dreams of becoming a musician. I have learned to understand speech by lip reading and I have learned to feel sound as if though my body were a giant ear.

So are our hopes and dreams the essence of what

makes us human? Or perhaps the key is strength of character and determination. Personally, I have certainly needed all of these traits throughout the journey of my life. But I also feel being open-minded is important. Open-mindedness leads us to information that allows us to make choices and decisions we might not otherwise have made.

It also brings about flexibility and adaptability. When I lost my hearing I chose to adapt and integrate myself into a mainstream school. From my perspective the choice was either to be pigeonholed as disabled or to find a way open up a new career as the world's first full time solo percussionist. I have never regretted my ability to make my own choices!

So what makes us human? Clearly the answer is complicated. I am reminded of another question that I am frequently asked: would I be better musician if I had not lost my hearing? I have no idea. But I do know life begins and ends with listening. Perhaps the fact that I have opened my body and my mind to a different way of listening enables me to be more sensitive. If other people learned to engage their bodies as a huge ear perhaps their idea of what makes us human would be affected too.

In conclusion, I feel that compassion, patience, inclusion, individuality and cultural awareness are all forms of social listening. To me, social listening is predominantly what makes us human.

Listen, world, to the sound of the universe

Listen listen listen.

My career and my life have been about listening in the deepest possible sense. Losing my hearing meant learning how to listen differently, to discover features of sound I hadn't realized existed. Losing my hearing made me a better listener.

So, harken world—there is sound, there is rhythm.

At the heart of every life form there is movement.

Flux. Change. The ancient Greeks knew it, the mediaeval saints lived it, the Christian gospels describe Jesus walking with rhythmic treads through the fields of corn or across the water.

Without oscillation movement there is nothing. Stability and solidity are illusions.

Everything oscillates, vibrates, from the bridges of steel or concrete and glass in church windows to the energy shells round atoms.

We recognise and experience our world through rhythm. Even colours oscillate at different frequencies. Everything vibrates, everything" 'speaks" in the great universe of sound.

So now I am workng towards establishing creating a centre that embodies my mission to improve communication and social cohesion by encouraging everyone to find new ways of listening. I want to inspire, to create, to engage and to empower.

I take every chance to speak (and I'm still invited a lot) and passionately about education, business, music and so on, drawing on my experience as an seem to succeed. For if we are in a measure divided by separate languages, there is always—and has been from the start of human society—a drum that can bring us together.

Within this great human I am so lucky now, at this particular point in human history, to be living in the beautiful countryside of Cambridgeshire in the east of England.

And to have such a great team to work with. They put it so perfectly (you too might chime in to this great mission) when they say,

In supporting Evelyn's multifaceted work we aim to 'Teach the World to Listen' through profound musical, educational and charitable/ social experiences. We aim to use the tools of performance, advocacy, consultancy and education to inspire active, receptive listening, both to ourselves and others.

We want to offer all people access to experiences and perspectives, offered by a host of experts, enabling us to 'Teach the World to Listen.'

So who are we doing it for?

Everyone.

Our work is for people today and for future generations, locally and internationally.

Everyone!

—and that includes you.

Whatever you do my warm wishes for a great and inspiring life.

You might also like ...

If you enjoyed this you might also like some of the following:

Internet links

www.evelyn.co.uk
My website (this has a full list, regularly updated, of my work, including my compositions, with web links to many of them and to my performances, some with videos)

www.allmusic.com/artist/evelyn-glennie-mn0000126390/compositions/

www.amazon.co.uk/Altamira-Mark-Knopfler/dp/B01D0WEGYK/

Youtube.com/watch?v=k067gEuEFJY

Books

Steven Feld, *Jazz Cosmopolitanism in Accra: Five Musical Years in Ghana*, Duke University Press, 2012.

Evelyn Glennie, *Good Vibrations*, Arrow Books, 1991.
(My Autobiography)

Rocky Maffit, *Rhythm and Beauty, The Art of Percussion*, Billboard Books, 2005.
(Includes among other things some stunning photos.)

References

John Blacking, *How Musical is Man?* University of Washington Press. 1974

Nicholas Cook, *Music: A Very Short introduction*, Oxford University Press, 2000.

Ruth Finnegan, *The Hidden Musicians. Music-Making in an English Town*, Wesleyan University Press, 2013.

J P Harper-Scott (ed.) *An Introduction to Music Studies*, Cambridge University Press, 2009.

Helen Keller, '*Letter*', The Auricle, 2,6, March 1924. Available through American Foundation for the Blind, Helen Keller Archives (online https://www.afb.org/blog/afb-blog/helen-keller-letter-on-beethoven's-ninth-symphony-goes-viral/12

Peter J Martin, *Sounds and Society*, Manchester University Press, 1997.

West African sansa (Sierra Leone *kututeng*), made and finger-played with somewhat Bachlike music by a village blacksmith using a biscuit box, locally smelted iron, and rattling stones (Ruth Finnegan, Kakarima 1961).

Preparing for the gruelling task of weeding the growing millet to the beat of the split drum made and played by the blacksmith musician Karanke Dema in northern Suerra Leone (Ruth Finnegan, 1961).

Fijian stamping and thudding poles dance.

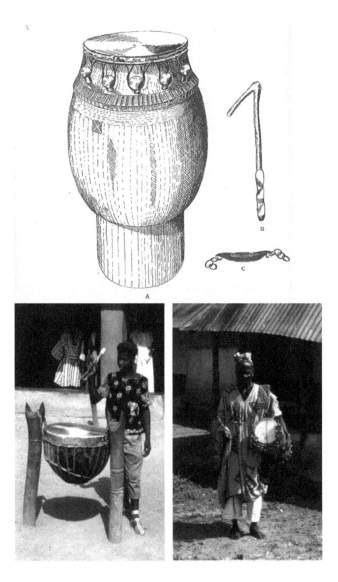

Sketch of nineteenth century Ghanaian drum.

Threashing sing Sierra Leone, the beating sticks at once coordinating practical implements and instruments for percussion (Ruth Finnegan 1961).

In all,cultures, it seems, rhythm and the patterned rhythms of dance are learned early. Whether in African villages (Ruth Finnegan, Sierra Leone, 1961), or American suburbs.

Questions for discussion, reflection, and action

Are you a musician? Well everyone is in a way, we all listen to music. So, rephrasing, are you involved in any kind of active music-making on your own or with a group, solo or collective, vocal or instrumental? If so what do you feel you get out of it?

Are you (or anyone you know) a percussionist in any shape or form? If so what do you think you (they) get out of that?

Would you agree with my idea that listening better would help,to bring us together (good subject for a discussion)?

Do the pictures in this book add to your understanding in any way(s)?

Do you think there are similarities between acting and music-making? If so, what are they, or if not , why do you think this?

Should everyone learn an instrument (another good subject for a debate)?

How many percussion instruments can you and/or your friends think of?

What, in your view, is music and why does it, or might it, matter?

What is the main thing you would say you have learned from this book? Do your friends agree? Your teacher? Any musicians you know?

Hearing Others' Voices

Hearing Others' Voices: A transcultural and transdisciplinary book series in simple and straightforward language, to inform and engage general readers, undergraduates and, above all, sixth formers in recent advances in thought, unaccountably overlooked areas of the world, and key issues of the day.

Lightning Source UK Ltd.
Milton Keynes UK
UKHW050200290619
345224UK00007B/43/P